If Animals Co

Dogs

If Animals Could Talk: Dogs is a revision of *What Are They Saying?: Dogs*, published in 2014
by Purple Toad Publishing, Inc. Reproduction of its contents is strictly prohibited without
written permission from the rights holder.

Paperback ISBN 979-8-89094-056-8

Hardback ISBN 979-8-89094-057-5

Library of Congress Control Number: 2023944061

To learn more about the other great books from Fox Chapel Publishing, or to find a retailer near you, call toll-free
800-457-9112 or visit us at *www.FoxChapelPublishing.com*.

We are always looking for talented authors. To submit an idea, please send a brief inquiry to
acquisitions@foxchapelpublishing.com.

Fox Chapel Publishing makes every effort to use environmentally friendly paper for printing.

Printed in China

If Animals Could Talk:

Dogs

Learn Fun Facts About the Things Dogs Do!

Ann Tatock

I am stretched out on the floor in a warm ray of sunshine. Since early morning, I have been very busy barking, eating, playing, and napping. Now it is time for the best moment of the day!

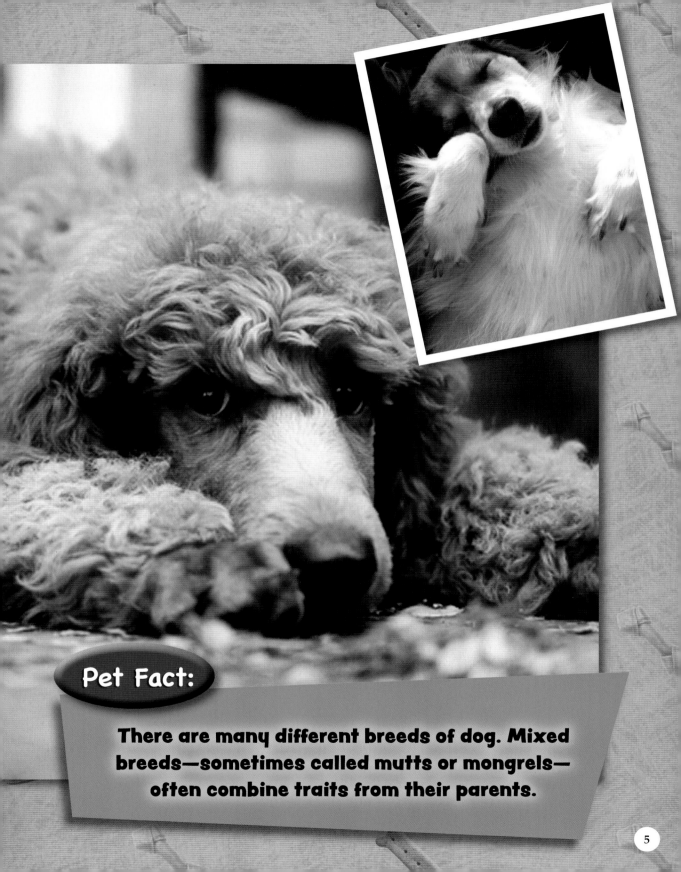

There are many different breeds of dog. Mixed breeds—sometimes called mutts or mongrels— often combine traits from their parents.

I lift my head, and my ears stand straight up. I hear the school bus stop in front of the house. I hear footsteps on the sidewalk. Someone opens the front door and calls my name. "Charlie!"

Pet Fact:

While dogs can't tell time, they have "internal clocks" that let them know when it's time for supper or when to expect their owners home.

"Here I am!" I say, though it sounds like "Yip, yip!" My tail wags so fast that my whole body dances. My best buddy calls it my Happy Dance.

Pet Fact:

A dog who is about to bite may wag its tail, too, but its body will be rigid and its tail pointing up.

I lick my buddy's cheek, which is how I say, "Welcome back! I missed you!"

Pet Fact:

Dogs are very loyal to their owners and offer them a lot of affection.

Now it's my turn for a little loving. I roll over to show my tummy. My eyes are closed and I'm relaxed, which means I want my buddy to pet there!

Pet Fact:

When a dog offers you its belly, it means it trusts you.

We go to the kitchen, where my buddy has a snack. "Don't forget me!" I say, but it sounds like "Yawp!" My friend smiles. "Sit," he says. I sit. He rewards me with a dog biscuit.

Pet Fact:

With patient training,
dogs can master many
tricks, such as shaking
paws, rolling over, and
sitting up to beg.

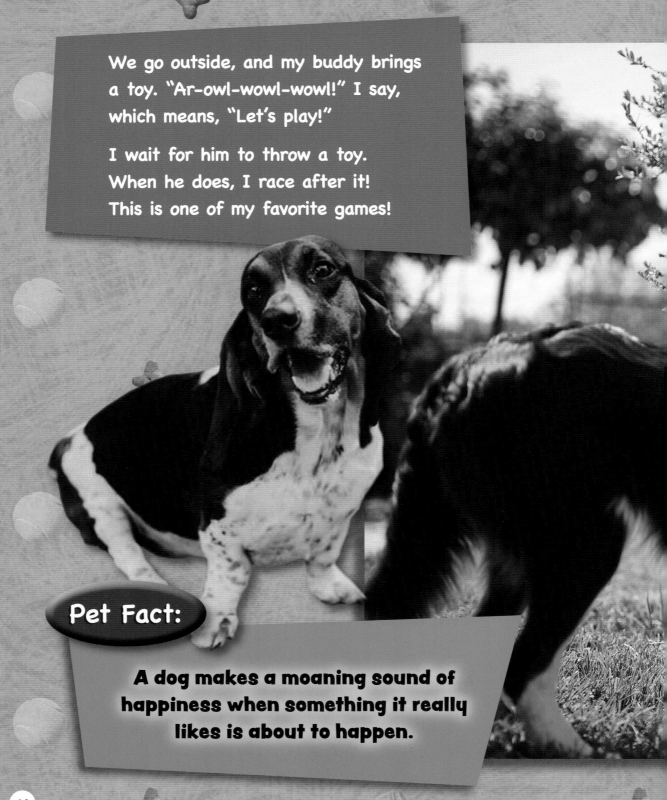

We go outside, and my buddy brings a toy. "Ar-owl-wowl-wowl!" I say, which means, "Let's play!"

I wait for him to throw a toy. When he does, I race after it! This is one of my favorite games!

Pet Fact:

A dog makes a moaning sound of happiness when something it really likes is about to happen.

I run across the yard. Suddenly I cry out, "Yelp!" I have stepped on a sharp pebble in the grass. But I am very brave. I keep on running to fetch the toy.

Pet Fact:

A dog whimpers or yelps
when it is in pain.

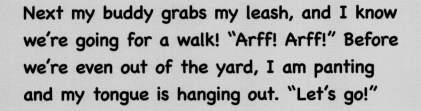

Next my buddy grabs my leash, and I know we're going for a walk! "Arff! Arff!" Before we're even out of the yard, I am panting and my tongue is hanging out. "Let's go!"

Pet Fact:

Dogs can't sweat like humans, so they pant to cool down. But dogs also pant when they are excited!

But wait! First I have to stop and smell everything. I explore my world with my nose.

Pet Fact:

A dog's sense of smell is 100 times stronger than yours!

Pet Fact:

Dogs like to roll on the ground to pick up the scent of other animals. They think it smells good, like canine (doggie) perfume!

When I smell something especially interesting, I roll in the grass until my buddy tugs at my leash and tells me to stop.

We walk and walk. It feels good to exercise and stretch my legs. A little dog walks toward us with her buddy. I must seem very big to her. She cowers with her tail between her legs.

With my front legs stretched forward and my wiggling rear end up in the air, I invite her to play. She knows I'm saying, "Let's be friends!"

Look at that dog across the street. He is soooo big! Now I'm the little guy. Just to be safe, I'll tug on the leash and scurry toward home, which means, "Come on, buddy!"

Pet Fact:

Dogs come in four sizes—small (sometimes called toy), medium, large, and giant.

After our walk, I need a bath. I guess I rolled in too much dirt! My buddy puts me in the tub and washes me clean with soapy water. Many dogs like baths, but I don't. I would rather run and play!

Pet Fact:

Grooming your dog includes bathing it, brushing its fur, and keeping its nails clipped.

At night, I am happy to curl up beside my best buddy's bed. He reaches over and scratches my ear. "Good night, Charlie," he says. "I love you." I sigh contentedly and close my eyes. It is good to be home. Good night.

BOOKS

Boynton, Sandra. *Doggies*. New York: Little
    Simon Publishing, 1984.

Day, Alexandra. *Good Dog Carl*.
    New York: Little Simon Publishing, 1996.

Gravett, Emily. *Dogs*. Douglas,
    Isle of Man: Pan Macmillan, 2009.

Priddy, Roger. *My Big Animal Book*. New York:
    St. Martin's Press, 2002.

Schindel, John. *Busy Doggies! A Busy Animals
    Book*. Berkeley, CA:
    Tricycle Press, 2003.

Van Fleet, Matthew. *Dog*. New York: Simon &
    Schuster, 2007.

WORKS CONSULTED

Bain, Terry. *You Are a Dog: Life Through the Eyes
    of Man's Best Friend*. New York: Harmony
    Books, 2004.

Davis, Caroline. *Essential Dog: The Ultimate
    Guide to Owning a Happy and Healthy Pet*.
    London: Octopus Publishing Group Ltd.,
    2006.

Fogle, Bruce. *Dog Owner's Manual*. New York:
    Dorling Kindersley, Inc., 2003.

Fogle, Bruce. *Dog: The Definitive Guide for Dog
    Owners*. Buffalo, NY: Firefly Books Inc., 2010.

Millan, Cesar. *A Member of the Family: Cesar
    Millan's Guide to a Lifetime of Fulfillment with
    Your Dog*. New York: Harmony Books, 2008.

ON THE INTERNET

Coren, Stanley, PhD. Psychology Today,
    "Canine Corner"
    http://www.psychologytoday.com/blog/
    canine-corner/

The Spruce Pets
    http://dogs.about.com/

Duncan, Deb. Come, Sit,
    Stay . . .Canine Etiquette
    www.thedogspeaks.com

Pet Place
    www.petplace.com